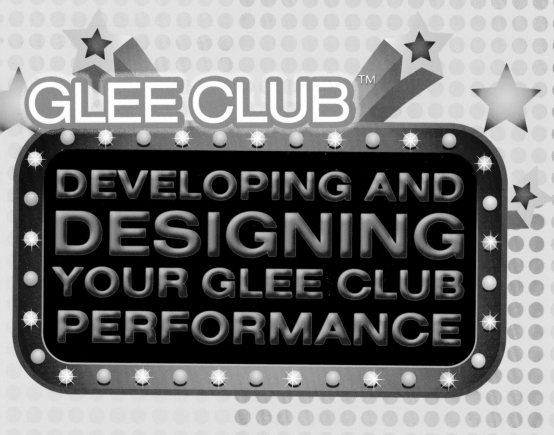

GLEE CLUB ™

DEVELOPING AND DESIGNING YOUR GLEE CLUB PERFORMANCE

ANASTASIA SUEN

ROSEN
PUBLISHING®

NEW YORK

Published in 2013 by The Rosen Publishing Group, Inc.
29 East 21st Street, New York, NY 10010

Copyright © 2013 by The Rosen Publishing Group, Inc.

First Edition

Library of Congress Cataloging-in-Publication Data

Suen, Anastasia.
Developing and designing your glee club performance/Anastasia Suen.—1st ed.
    p. cm.—(Glee club)
Includes bibliographical references and index.
ISBN 978-1-4488-6877-3 (library binding)—
ISBN 978-1-4488-6881-0 (pbk.)—
ISBN 978-1-4488-6882-7 (6-pack)
1. Glee clubs. I. Title.
MT930.S84 2012
792.702'22—dc23

                                                                    2012003288

Manufactured in the United States of America

CPSIA Compliance Information: Batch #S12YA: For further information, contact Rosen Publishing, New York, New York, at 1-800-237-9932.

CONTENTS

INTRODUCTION 4

CHAPTER 1   PUTTING ON A SHOW 7

CHAPTER 2   IT STARTS WITH THE MUSIC 16

CHAPTER 3   MAKING IT A PERFORMANCE 26

CHAPTER 4   FUND-RAISING 36

CHAPTER 5   SHOWTIME 47

GLOSSARY 54

FOR MORE INFORMATION 55

FOR FURTHER READING 58

BIBLIOGRAPHY 60

INDEX 62

INTRODUCTION

You've probably seen the show *Glee* on television. A group of high school students have a club that sings and dances. They break into song almost everywhere they go. They perform on stage as musicians accompany them.

What you may not know is that the glee club is a long-standing high school and college tradition. Glee clubs have been performing in the United States since the mid-1800s. The Harvard Glee Club, started in 1858, was the first glee club in the United States. The following year, students at the University of Michigan formed a glee club. Other colleges soon followed.

The Yale Glee Club, started in 1863, had its first overseas concert tour in 1928. Over the years, it has performed on six different continents. It tours during spring and summer breaks.

The television show *Glee*, shown here, is a big hit and inspired many high schools to start their own glee clubs. Now it's your turn!

The very first glee clubs were all male, as only men attended those colleges. These male choruses sang a cappella, which means they sang without any instrumental accompaniment. *Cappella* is the Italian word for "chapel," and this was how they sang in the chapel at this time. They sang with voices only.

So where did the name "glee" come from? In eighteenth-century England a glee was a song with different voice parts sung by three or more unaccompanied voices. So it's a song, but it's more. "Glee" is also the word for mirth, a happy joyful feeling. Put those two together, and you have a glee club.

Seeing college students perform choral music inspired high school students. The glee club tradition moved down to the high school level. In high school, the glee club is also known by another name, show choir. A show choir puts on a show, with song, dance, and instruments. You can start one at your school, too!

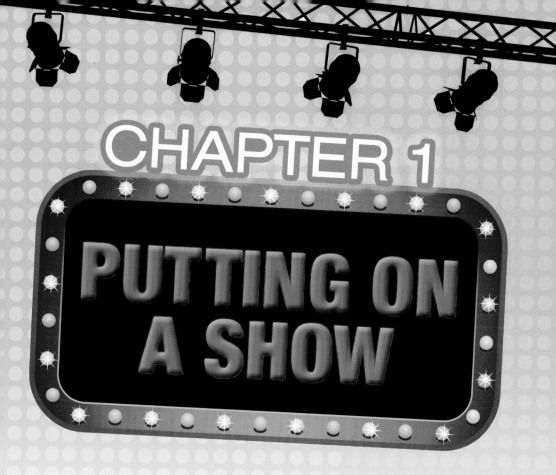

CHAPTER 1

PUTTING ON A SHOW

Yes, you can start your own glee club, and this book will show you how. You'll find out what you need to do to make your dream of having a glee club in your high school a reality. In some ways, a glee club is like any other club. It takes someone working behind the scenes to make it happen. That person is you!

Think about it. Every show has performers. The camera focuses on them. The audience does, too. The performers are in the spotlight.

But who is behind the spotlight? Who is making the show a reality? Someone has to do all of the work that makes a show

7

Working together, the members of your new glee club can bring a show to life. With singing, dancing, musicians, and a stage crew, you can bring it all together.

happen. Someone has to bring that show to life. Someone has to select the music, hold auditions, and choose the singers, musicians, and stage crew. Getting everyone to work together is the next task and it's a big one. Your glee club will be performing at different venues with new music and choreography throughout the entire school year.

In the entertainment business, the person who makes it all happen is called the producer. The producer is the one who sees the big picture. He or she has an idea and then makes that idea come to life. The producer oversees the entire project. He or she does that by hiring others to pay close attention to each and every little detail.

Those details are the focus of this book. We will begin with the big idea—forming a glee club—and then move to the specifics. Step-by-step, you'll learn what you have to do to organize a year of glee club performances.

You Can Produce a Show

First, let's look at the big idea. What do you want to do? Where do you want to end up? Do you see yourself performing on stage, singing and dancing with a group of friends with spotlights on you as musicians play behind you? Close your eyes and imagine it. Now, how can you make that happen?

Stephen Covey, author of the best-selling book *The 7 Habits of Highly Effective People* says that everything is created twice. First you create it in your mind, and then you make it happen in the real world. It takes two steps to make things happen. It might seem faster just to start working, but it's not. When you want to build something, things flow more smoothly if you make a plan first.

Professional athletes use this two-step process to make it to the top. Before the competition, athletes close their eyes and sees themselves performing. They visualize the entire performance in their minds. They see themselves making all the moves step-by-step. Then they open their eyes and make it happen.

"Begin with the End in Mind" is what Covey calls this process. He recommends that you begin each day, task, or project with a vision of what you want. After you visualize it, then you take the steps to make that dream a reality.

What People Do You Need?

You want to form a glee club. That is your dream, your goal. Now who do you need to help you make that happen? Close your eyes and see yourself on the stage again. Who else was there with you?

Did you see…

1. Singers and dancers?
2. Musicians?
3. A stage crew?

You need people to sing and dance. You need people to play the music. You also need people to get the show ready to be seen. To form a glee club, you need lots of different people with varied skills. Let's talk about the three areas of glee club.

Singers and Dancers

Your singers will also be dancing, so it's a "two in one" position. Who sings what will depend on who joins. That will determine how many voice parts your group will have. Will it be two parts (melody and harmony), three parts (soprano, alto, and bass), or four parts (soprano, alto, tenor, and bass)? There is no way of knowing ahead of time. This is something you will discover after auditions.

Rehearsal is vital to any glee club performance. It helps to polish your performance. Make sure you practice together at least twice a week.

Musicians

Some glee clubs perform a cappella. Some groups do this for all of their songs, while others save this vocals-only approach for special songs during their performance.

If your glee club competes in an invitational, you must have a backup band.

For these competitive show choir events, the members of the band must also be high school students. (Only one adult band member is permitted at competitive events.)

POTENTIAL GLEE CLUB POSITIONS

Like any club, you will want to have elections for these positions:

Elected Officers:

- President
- Vice President
- Secretary/Historian
- Treasurer
- Publicist

You will also need to have someone in charge of these singing and dancing positions:

Appointed Positions:

- Soprano Section Leader
- Alto Section Leader
- Tenor Section Leader
- Bass Section Leader
- Girls Dance Captain
- Boys Dance Captain
- Crew Chief

As your glee club becomes more active, you may want to delegate these positions:

Optional Positions:

- Fund-raising Director
- Booking Agent
- Travel Agent
- Costume Director

When you are performing at school or a private event, you may use musicians of any age. Just like you do in music class, you can sing while someone plays the piano. Adding drums will help keep everyone on beat. Guitars and other stringed instruments, such as a cello or an upright bass, can also accompany you. The band director at your school can help you find musicians to perform with your club.

A Stage Crew

Once you get close to performance time, you'll need to recruit members for your stage crew. The stage crew takes care of the technical and mechanical aspects of the theater performance. They take care of the set, lights, sound, props, and costumes.

What Materials Do You Need?

Yes, you need people to make your glee club show a reality. You also need materials, like sheet music, musical instruments, and a stage. And last but not least, you need publicity. No one can come to your show if they don't know about it, and that includes the people you envision performing on the stage.

To make your show a reality, you need three very different things: people, materials, and publicity. These three things are very closely intertwined. You can't have just one of them. You need all three at once.

If you do the work and get all three into place, you'll have a show to put on. An audience will come to see you and then it will really be a show! And one show will lead to another. After all, you didn't start a glee club to produce a single event. A glee club performs the entire school year.

Your glee club adviser can help you with every aspect of developing and designing your performance: setting rehearsals, picking music, choosing a choreographer, and more.

Performing in public can lead to performing at private events. Your club can be paid for performing at birthday parties, weddings, and holiday parties. Why not?

How Can You Get the Word Out?

To make your glee club a reality, you will need to do what any producer does. You need to gather a group of people who will work together. The only difference is that you're working with volunteers. You can't just get on the phone and call a few agents. You have to find all of the talent yourself. To do that, you need to get the word out.

Go school-wide with your publicity. Write up a short paragraph for morning announcements and the school newspaper. Ask for permission to post flyers in the hallways. Talk to the music teachers at school and ask them to mention it in all of their classes.

Share the word with social media. Use Myspace or Facebook. Send out a message on Twitter.

Ask local businesses that cater to students if you can put up posters. Send your announcements to the upcoming events section of the local newspaper or television station. The news media is always looking for local stories to cover. Why not give them the opportunity to share yours?

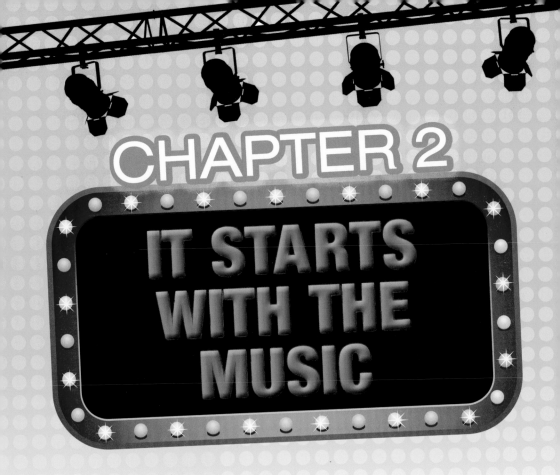

CHAPTER 2

IT STARTS WITH THE MUSIC

Music is at the heart of any glee club. Great music and people who love music are what make glee club so much fun. Let's see how you can put those two together as you work to make your glee club a reality.

A Music Department Mentor

In most high schools, you need to have a faculty member adviser for your club. The glee club is no exception. Ask someone in the music department to be your mentor. Someone who works with music all day will be a great resource for you.

You want to find songs that help you connect with the audience. A memorable song has emotion and great lyrics. It tells a story that audiences can enjoy.

Selecting Songs

Song selection is an important part of any glee club performance. You want to select songs that your glee club members know. At the same time, it's important to find songs with sheet music for the different voice parts already arranged. That way you won't have to write your own scores.

Your local music store will have sheet music for many vocal arrangements. Depending on what voice arrangements you will be using in your choir, you'll need music with two parts, three parts, or all four voice parts (soprano, alto, tenor, bass). For auditions, choose sheet music with all four voice parts.

WORKING WITH A MENTOR

The role of a mentor is not to do your work for you. A mentor is there to help you figure out how to do the work by yourself. Your mentor has already "been there, done that" so he or she can guide you as you try it yourself for the first time. A mentor is also someone that you can ask questions. Sometimes you need to talk things through to figure out what to do next.

Try to meet with your mentor on a regular basis. This will help to keep the lines of communication open. Talking about things before you try them can help you prevent problems. It can also help you brainstorm new ideas.

Permissions

When you pay for your sheet music, you are also paying for the right to perform that music at your events. However, if you sell copies of your performance, then you need to pay for performance rights. If you make money on the music, then the original creators get a piece of the pie, too. That's the law.

Setting Up Auditions

Glee club is more than just singing. It's singing and dancing at the same time. This means you will need to select two types of songs for your audition music. You will need one song for a vocal solo and another for singing while dancing. (You may wish to select a different song for the male and female parts.)

During auditions, you'll be in front of several judges, who will be listening to you sing and seeing how well you know the routine. Practicing before an audition is vital.

Finding Judges for Auditions

Use a panel of judges for your auditions. This ensures that the auditions are fair and balanced, and that the tryouts won't be a popularity contest. An uneven number of judges (three, five, or seven) will eliminate any tie votes. Ask your glee club mentor to serve as a judge. Other members of the music department may also want to be judges. To help you judge the dancing, ask someone from the theater department and any local dance instructors that you know. A faculty member who was in glee club can help you, too.

Judging can be fairly subjective, so use a rubric, which is a set of rules to follow, just like your teachers do. Ask your mentor to help you find or develop one. A rubric will give your judges specific things to look for during auditions. It makes the selection process more objective. Some of the students who audition will be better at singing while others will be better at dancing. The judges will have to consider both skills.

Preparing for Auditions

After you have selected your judges, you will need to find a room as well as a date and time for your auditions. Coordinating schedules is always a difficult task. You may decide to have several days for auditions so that you can accommodate both the schedules of your judges and the students.

Something else you may want to consider is having an audition workshop before the auditions. During the audition workshop you (and/or your music and dance mentors) can teach potential glee club members the song they will be singing and the dance moves you would like them to perform. Having everyone perform the same routine makes it easier for the students to prepare. It also makes it easier for the judges, because they are comparing the same moves.

If you are not able to hold an audition workshop, you can upload audio files of the songs for students to listen to before the audition. Some glee clubs also create a YouTube video of the songs and dances they want the students to perform. Your auditioners will have to buy their own sheet music, but having an audio file to listen to is very helpful.

Casting Call Publicity

Spread the word far and wide about your auditions so you can create a fabulous glee club. Write up a short paragraph for morning announcements and a longer one for the school newspaper. Ask the front office for permission to put fliers around the school.

For all of your publicity, list the time, date, and location of the auditions. Remember to include the names of the songs the students will be performing, as well as places they can buy the sheet music.

If you have created any audio and video files, upload a link to the files online. Ask the music teacher if you can add a glee club page to the school's Web page. Or set up a Facebook or Myspace page on your own. Setting up an online presence now will give you an easy way to communicate with everyone quickly, before and after the auditions.

It's best to get the word out two to four weeks ahead of time. That will give students time to prepare for their auditions.

Get the word out about your glee club in as many ways as you can—online, in the school paper, and in morning announcements. Reach out to the entire community.

It will also give you time to spread the word. People don't always remember things they hear once. You have to repeat your message over and over and over. It's what marketers call the Rule of Seven. A person may have to hear your message seven times before they decide to take action.

Selecting Vocalists

After each student has auditioned, you and your judges will have the task of selecting vocalists for your glee club. Some glee clubs have an open door policy and everyone who auditions is accepted. Other glee clubs insist on certain standards of performance and select only the strongest singers and dancers for their club. Talk to your mentor about which approach would work best for you.

Selecting Student Section Leaders

Your judges will help you decide which singers belong in each vocal category. The next step is to select a section leader for each voice part: soprano, alto, tenor, and bass. The role of the section leader is to help organize all the singers for that vocal part. Each section leader will make sure that everyone in their section has their music. They will also be in charge of any extra practices for their part.

Finding Musicians

Now that you have your singers all lined up, it's time to find the musicians to back you up. Who you need will depend on where you are performing. If you're going to perform in a competition, the instrumentalists must be other high school

Other students at your school can help you bring your show to life. Ask student musicians to back you up as you perform. It will make you all sound great!

students. That's the rule. If you are performing at a private party, you may be able to use adults or college students as your musicians.

The type of music you will be performing is another important consideration. Big band music needs brass to back it up, while jazz sounds best with an upright bass. If your school has a band and/or an orchestra, then you are in luck! Talk to the band director at your school about your music and see whom he or she recommends. Ask the orchestra director for help. If your school has instrumental ensembles, these groups of student musicians may be able to accompany you on a regular basis. They want to perform and you want to perform. It's a winning combination!

Practice, Practice, Practice

Now that you have singers and musicians, they all need to practice. Everyone needs time to learn the music. Solo practice leads to mastery, but you will be performing with others, so group practice is important, too. Each section needs to practice together, and the entire ensemble needs to practice together as well. Set up a regular practice time, twice a week. Some clubs practice in the morning before school, but most practice after school twice a week.

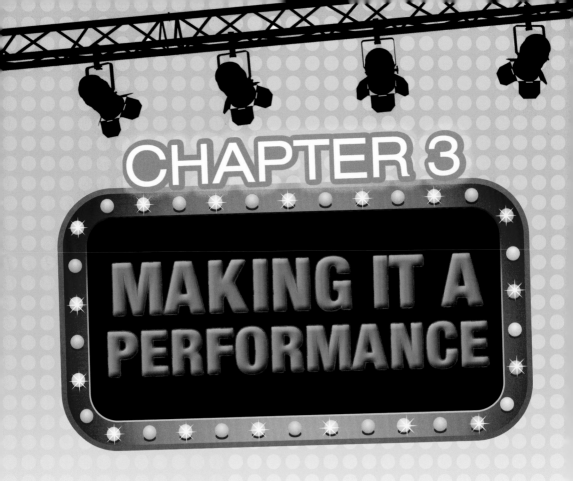

CHAPTER 3

MAKING IT A PERFORMANCE

Once you have the music ready to go, it's time to add choreography. A choreographer will create a dance routine for your singers. Having your singers move while they perform makes your show more interesting to watch. It brings your performance to the next level.

Just as you did for your singing, ask an adult to act as a mentor for your choreography. How will you find a choreographer? Some of your glee club members might already be working with a choreographer. Do you have a theater and dance department at your school? Is there a local dance company in your town? Are there any dance studios nearby?

You'll want to move as you sing. Sometimes a simple hand movement is best; other times you need to move your entire body and dance.

Many students have been studying dance since they were in preschool. Using a connection that you already have is easier than calling someone up out of the blue.

Another possibility is to look for "graduates" of other glee clubs. Former glee club members who are college students may have flexible schedules. One of them may be able to help you. After college, some former glee club members work as choreographers for hire.

Working on Choreography

A choreographer will help your singers move as they perform. What type of dance moves the choreographer decides to use will depend on the song and how it is performed.

DIY CHOREOGRAPHY

If you can't find a choreographer, or you don't have the funds to pay for one, you can always do it yourself. Yes, your glee club members can create their own choreography. You don't have to go it alone. Let the small screen inspire you. Television and the Internet will help you choreograph your own performance.

Many glee clubs have uploaded videos of their performances on YouTube. Use the search engine on the YouTube Web site to help you find them. If you type the words "glee club" you'll see videos from the television show *Glee*. If you use the search words "show choir" you'll see performances from other high schools around the country. (There are over nineteen thousand to choose from now, and that number will only keep growing.)

Is the song sung by the entire group? Or does it have alternating voices or solos? When the singers alternate, the ones who are singing may be the focus of the dance at that point. Or the others may be dancing while the soloist stands still. These are decisions the choreographer makes.

Dance Captains

Just as you had vocal section leaders, you also need dance leaders. Appoint two dance captains, one male and one female. These dance captains will work closely with your dance mentor or choreographer. They will help the members of your glee club learn and practice their dance routines.

After the choreographer decides on the dance moves, there are two important steps: learning and cleaning. The learning step is obvious. Your members will learn the dance steps. In the cleaning step, your members will perfect their moves, as individuals and a group.

The dance captain will oversee additional practices after the choreographer leaves. Sometimes the girls will practice together, and sometime the boys will practice together. Eventually, the entire group will need to practice together. (Some clubs go away for a choreography weekend to practice their routines.) Because of the importance of this role, most clubs select a dance captain with dance experience. In some glee clubs, this position is reserved only for seniors.

Finding Your Way on the Stage

During the year you will perform in many different locations. Not every stage is the same size, so you will have to adjust your choreography accordingly. Use the trick that actors use. Make a map of where you will move on the stage.

Deciding where to move on a stage is called blocking. Each part of the stage floor has a different name. These names indicate where you stand on the stage as you look toward the audience.

The dance captains should keep a record of who moves where for each number. This record can be written or visual. Choreographers use a formal system called labanotation to show which part of the body moves in which direction movement by movement. It's like writing a musical score for the body.

After each person learns his or her dance moves individually, it's time to practice as a group. You don't want to bump into one another!

You will probably find it easier to use choreographer Jody Sperling's methods. As she creates a dance, she works with her dancers to give each part of the dance a name. Formal names are not used. Instead, each move is named for how it looks or feels, using names like "Rainbow" and "The Butterfly." Sperling makes a video of the dance and uses the YouTube annotation tool to label the moves.

By recording the dance moves for each number, your dance captain will have an easy-to-access record for future practices. Members can use the videos to practice at home. This visual record will help everyone see what the dance looks like from the audience's point of view.

STAGE POSITIONS

	Upstage Right	Upstage Center	Upstage Left	
Right Wing	Center Right	Center Stage	Center Left	Left Wing
	Downstage Right	Downstage Center	Downstage Left	

Curtain   Curtain

Working the Stage

When you are performing on stage, you also need a stage crew. A stage crew takes care of everything that goes on the stage before, during, and after the performance. They also take care of the front-of-the-house management: collecting tickets and helping people find their seats. (Think theater ushers.) This is another set of volunteers for you to organize.

Crew Chief

The volunteer in charge of the stage crew is called the crew chief. The crew chief's tasks change as the date draws closer

31

to the production. Before the show begins, the focus will be on creating the set. As time for the show draws near, the focus will change. The crew chief will make sure that there are volunteers to handle the front-of-the-house management and all of the backstage matters.

A few weeks before the show, the stage crew will build the set for your performance. Most sets are built from scratch using wood and paint, so you need volunteers that are handy with tools. These volunteers also need to be able to do heavy lifting because large wooden sets are heavy.

Your stage crew needs to be handy with tools (and good with math) to build your sets from scratch. Students taking shop class may be willing to help.

Any props that you need are also the responsibility of the stage crew. They will locate these items and take care of them before, during, and after the performance. The stage crew will make sure that the props appear on stage when they are needed.

The stage crew will also handle the workings of the stage itself. This includes the curtains, the lights, and the sound. If you are performing in a theater outside of school, there may be a stage crew on staff that will handle the curtains, lights, and sound. Your stage crew will need to communicate with

WORKING WITH VOLUNTEERS

To bring your show to life, you will be working with a lot of volunteers. The more collaborative you make the process, the easier it will be. Basically, people want to work with you if they have a say in what happens. If you insist on making all of the decisions yourself, you may find it hard to get things done. A better method is to talk things over and make decisions as a group.

If you have delegated responsibility for each part of the performance, then there will be someone to make sure that each and every little thing gets done. Trust the person that you've asked to take charge of each area of responsibility. If people feel that they are really in charge, then things will happen. The work will get done.

Delegating spreads out the responsibility and gives you less work to do. Working as a team makes everyone feel like they are important. (Because they are!) Your job is to communicate constantly about what is happening. That is how any big project is completed. As the saying goes, "Many hands make light work."

the theater staff about the sound, lighting, and curtain cues for your performance.

If you are performing in a competition, your stage crew will also be timed for the work that they do. Each group is allotted only a certain amount of time to set up and perform. This includes moving the risers into the position your glee club prefers. If you need to use props during the competition, your stage crew will be in the wings to hand them out when they're needed. After the performance, the stage crew will gather everything up and put it away. Transportation and storage of sets and props are also the stage crew's responsibility.

Costumes and Makeup

Choosing costumes to wear during your performance is another decision that will have to be made. Finances play a large part

Stage makeup will help the audience see your facial movements from far away. You may want to designate one volunteer, or group of volunteers, to apply makeup to everyone.

in this decision. It costs money to buy costumes for everyone to wear. Some glee clubs wear street clothes when they sing. It can be as simple as everyone wearing black pants and a white long sleeved shirt. When everyone matches, it makes you look like a group. That makes it the perfect costume.

As time goes on, however, some clubs prefer to have costumes that look more like Broadway or Hollywood. Shiny satin and sequins stand out on the stage. So does stage makeup. At this point, you may need more volunteers to help put it all together. The stage crew chief may be in charge of the costumes and makeup, or you may decide to have a costume crew and/or a hair and makeup crew. The costume crew will be in charge of organizing the costumes for the entire crew. They will also be backstage to help with fittings and costume changes between songs. Each performer will be in charge of his or her hair and makeup, but there will be someone on hand to help if needed.

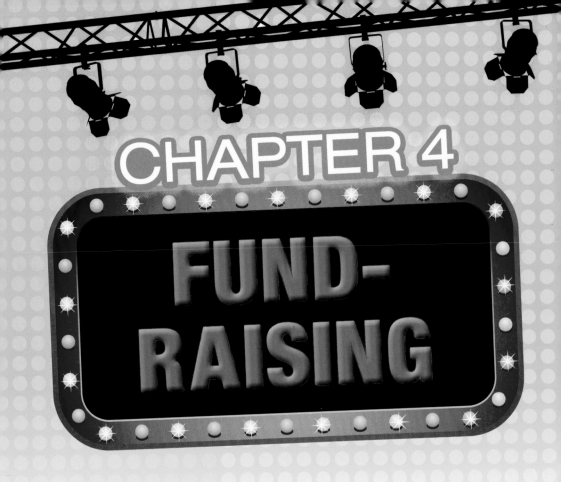

CHAPTER 4

FUND-RAISING

Fund-raising is another important matter for your glee club. You need money to pay for contest entry fees as well as costumes and travel expenses. Your costs will be ongoing throughout the school year. You may need to do fund-raising all year.

Everyone in the glee club will participate in fund-raising, but you will need two key people to help you manage it. Most clubs have a treasurer, a person who was elected by club members to manage the club's funds. The treasurer is the club's bookkeeper. He or she will keep a record of all of the

Your treasurer will manage your funds so that you have enough money to pay for what you need. This is a good position for someone who likes math.

monies coming in and going out. The monies coming in will be the funds that you raise with your fund-raising. The monies going out will pay for contest entry fees and facility use fees. Yes, sometimes you need to pay simply to show up. And to get there, you need to pay for your travel expenses. This is especially important if you are traveling out of your area. Do you need to pay for airfare? Will you need to rent a bus to get there? Will you need extra costumes to wear at each performance? All these costs add up.

The treasurer manages the funds, but you may also want to ask someone to be in charge of fund-raising itself. Name a fund-raising director. Now you have someone who is always thinking about the next fund-raiser.

IT'S UP TO YOU!

When you were in elementary school and middle school, parents were in charge of fund-raising. Now that you are in high school, everything changes. Now you are in charge of your own fund-raising. In high school, funds are raised by the club's members, not the parents. If parents want to raise funds, they must form a booster club.

Booster clubs have a place in high school, but they are controlled by parents and have their own rules. They must follow school district regulations as well as city, county, and state laws.

Your glee club is under the umbrella of the school district. Any funds that you raise should be put in the bank for you by the office manager or school bookkeeper. You are not required to open a bank account or to pay taxes. This allows you to focus on the glee club instead.

Asking for Direct Donations

There are many different ways to raise money. One way is to ask businesses to sponsor your club. So why would someone just give you money? They give money to support what you do, but they also want something else. They want their donation to be acknowledged.

You can set up a glee club sponsorship program with set dollar amounts for different sponsorship levels. You would acknowledge your sponsor at each program by listing the

Begin at home and ask your family to support the glee club. They will see the results of all your hard work when you invite them to your show!

names of all of your sponsors on the back of your glee club programs.

Who would you ask to sponsor you? Begin at home and ask your family to sponsor the glee club. Ask your parents to see if their employer can sponsor the glee club. Sponsoring local groups is considered good advertising for companies. It shows that they are giving back to their community.

Ask local businesses to sponsor you, too. A business sponsorship can involve goods or services instead of a direct cash donation. Ask local grocery stores or florists if they can provide flowers for the stage. Grocery stores can also provide food in the lobby. Let everyone know who your sponsors are by thanking them on stage and in your printed program.

Asking for Volunteers

A tried-and-true fund-raising tactic is to have the members of your club volunteer to sell a product or a service. A product is something that is used by the consumer, such as cookie dough, taffy, or gourmet coffee. A service is something that you do for a consumer, like wash their car.

What type of fund-raiser would your glee club like to have? Share some possible choices and ask them what they would like to do. Your fund-raiser will go more smoothly when your members play an active part in the decision-making process.

At the same time, you also need to be aware of what else is going on in your school. The good news is, now that you're in high school you can manage your own glee club fund-raiser. The bad news is that every other club at your high school is also having fund-raisers. If you are not careful, two clubs may end up having the same fund-raiser at the same time. When that happens, both clubs earn less.

How can you find out what the other clubs are doing? As you plan each new fund-raiser, ask your members. Many of them are in other clubs as well. Ask the school office manager what he or she knows about upcoming fund-raisers. Better safe than sorry.

Approved Vendors

Another important thing to ask the office manager about is who you are allowed to work with when you raise funds. Some school districts have "approved" vendors. Each fund-raising company must have approval to work in the school district. They must fill out paperwork and meet all of the requirements of the school district before they can work there. These requirements include a history of honest business dealings and taking responsibility for their own merchandise. They must also supply proof of insurance.

Even if the school does not require that vendors meet their approval ahead of time, do your homework and check the vendors out. Make sure they meet your approval. Find out what others say about the company. Type their name into a search engine and see what kind of customer reviews they have. What do previous customers say about them? Do they respond in a timely manner? Do they replace defective products? If the company you work with has poor customer service, it makes you look bad, too. You're doing this to raise money for your club, not to add more work to your already busy schedule!

Profits and Losses

How will you make money with a fund-raising company? A percentage of the funds you collect will be yours to keep. Depending on the company and product, your cut will be 30 to 55 percent. This looks good on paper, but how does it work in real life?

Look carefully at the fine print. When does the fund-raising company want you to send in the money? Do you send it in before you take any customer orders, or afterward? In other words, are you their real customer? Or are you providing temporary sales staff for the company? This tiny item of fine print can turn your potential profits into a loss.

Most companies require that you pay for items before they ship them. But what if you can't sell everything you order? What do you do with the rest? Can you send it back? Or does the club just take a loss?

It's much better to sell the items first with an order form and then collect the money for them. Many fund-raising companies operate this way. You don't send them any money until you purchase something. This protects you and the company. The company sends you only what your customers want to buy. There are no extra items that need to be shipped back or kept as a loss.

Low Cost Fund-Raisers

When you work with a fund-raising company, you agree to split the funds you collect with that company. When you can create your own product or service, you don't have to share

SCHOOL BAKE SALE CHECKLIST

- Get permission from the front office to host the sale.
- Ask the custodian to set out a table for you.
- Cover the table with a tablecloth.
- Place the food on the table by types: cookies, brownies, cupcakes, etc.
- Make small price signs for each type. (Multiples of 25 cents are best.)
- Tape up flyers announcing your fund-raiser (on the table and in the hallways nearby).
- Use a cash box with plenty of change.
- Have a calculator for your cashiers to use (just in case).
- Place a stack of napkins on each end of the table.
- Put small paper plates and plastic forks and knives near any cakes and pies for sale.
- Have plenty of volunteers.

Having a bake sale at back-to-school functions helps you and your supporters. You advertise the glee club and raise money, and your supporters get a tasty treat!

the money you raise. This is why so many clubs have bake sales, car washes, and garage sales. To hold a clubwide garage sale, you just have to look for stuff in your garage and find a time and a place to sell the items. For a car wash, you need only car washing supplies and a local business that will let you use its site. Bake sale items are made by your members, at no cost to the club. You don't need to spend a lot of money for these popular fund-raisers.

Where Does the Money Go?

Each school has its own system for keeping track of funds that school clubs raise. This policy is usually set by the school district, and it is for your protection. Why do all of that work so someone can help themselves to your hard-earned cash?

A school club is under the supervision of the school, so the school handles the banking. This means there are rules about how it will be done. After you collect the money for your fund-raiser, it will be handed over to either your adviser or directly to someone in the front office. The office manager or the school bookkeeper will deposit the money into the bank for you. How much money you have in your glee club account will be recorded.

Your club needs to keep its own records, too. In fact, the school bookkeeper may require it. Everyone who works with numbers double-checks them, so he or she will want you to have checked all of your numbers before you turn in any money. You will also need to know how much money needs to be sent to the fund-raising company. If your group keeps 50 percent of the profit, how much will that be? Where does the check need to go? What is the address? What name do you write on the check? Your club treasurer needs to take care of all of these details.

Spreading the News About Your Fund-Raiser

Each time you have a new fund-raiser, you will need to publicize it. This is a job for your publicist. A publicist will spread the news about your fund-raising and your performances.

There are two kinds of publicity, internal and external. Letting your glee club members know about your next fund-raiser is internal publicity. Their support is essential to making any event happen. How can you help? Consider having a fund-raising incentive for your club members. Set up a bar graph or "thermometer" to show how much money has been raised. Have a contest between members to see who can raise the most money.

Most fund-raising groups recommend that you have a short window for your fund-raising event. Two weeks is the recommended amount of time for a fund-raiser that requires door-to-door selling. If you're having a "live" event where people need to come and buy something from you, be clear about when the event begins and ends. What day of the week will it take place? What time will it happen? Is there anything that needs to be done ahead of time?

The second type of publicity is external publicity. This is when you let the public know about your new fund-raising event. What type of publicity you use depends on where the fund-raising will take place. If you are having an in-school event, you will need to publicize the event only inside the school. Write up a short blurb about your event for morning announcements and the school newsletter. Ask for permission to put up flyers around school.

For events that take place on school property, such as the clubwide garage sale, place signs outside along the road. This will help passersby find your sale. Inside the building you will need to provide directional signs so that nonstudents can find you.

When you are having a fund-raising event outside school, publicize the event to the entire community. If you are having a car wash, it's as simple as setting up "Glee Club Car Wash" signs along the street. Put a sign facing each direction so that drivers from both sides of the street can see what you are doing.

If you are going door-to-door to raise funds, the best type of publicity is simply being a good neighbor. Neighbors are more likely to support your fund-raisers if you are friendly to them in your everyday life. It's like the old saying, "What goes around comes around."

CHAPTER 5

SHOWTIME

Most glee clubs perform throughout the school year. There are so many places you can sing! Your glee club can perform at schools, nursing homes, and private events like birthday and holiday parties. You can also perform at glee club competitions, called invitationals.

Performing at School

Performing at school will help you showcase your glee club to the other students at your high school. Your glee club can perform at open house or back to school night. It can also perform at other school functions where parents are invited. Having music at an event is a nice touch.

Practicing twice a week throughout the school year will help you develop your sound. Rehearsing with a piano will help you stay on key.

When you plan out your schedule for the year, be sure to include a school concert in the spring. This will help you recruit new members for the next school year. You need to do this every year because your seniors will graduate, leaving you with spaces to fill.

Ask the middle school if you can perform there, too. This will introduce your club to incoming freshman. You want them to think about joining you in the upcoming year.

Schedule a final spring concert near the end of the semester. This concert will serve as a "thank you and good-bye" concert for your graduating seniors. It will be nice to perform together one last time.

Volunteer Gigs

During the school year, you will also have many opportunities to sing as a volunteer. This is one way that you can give back to the community. You can sing at the local shopping center during the winter holidays. You can visit nursing homes and hospitals to perform for service hours. You can perform at functions for nonprofit groups, like the Junior League.

Paid Gigs

Once the word gets out about your glee club, you'll be asked to sing at birthday and holiday parties. Why not? This is great experience for your members. To

The members of your glee club can perform anywhere people want to hear music, whether it's a casual or formal performance. Music can make any occasion more festive.

smooth out the process, you may want to designate someone as your booking agent. This person would be in charge of organizing off-campus performances.

Depending on the venue, you may also need to bring your own musicians. They can be students or adults. See who is available.

When you perform at a private event, it is customary to be paid. How the money is distributed needs to be worked out ahead of time. How much will each person be paid? Will you split the money with musicians fifty-fifty? Will the money for the singers go to the club or to each performer? What will you do if not everyone in glee club is able to perform at that event?

There are no right or wrong answers. The important thing is to talk everything through before you go so everyone will know what to expect. (This is why adults always sign contracts before they begin work.)

Invitationals

Invitationals are competitions for glee clubs. Each glee club is given a set time, usually thirty minutes, to perform. During your time, you have to set up, perform several musical numbers, and take down any sets or equipment. Then, the next group gets the stage.

Invitationals take place at a large arena or performing arts hall. Glee clubs from far and wide will come to perform. Each group will have time to rehearse on the stage before the competition begins.

The competition itself is usually divided into two parts, preliminaries and finals. During both parts of the competition, every aspect of your performance will be given points. The judges, called adjudicators, will be looking at how long it takes to set up and take down the stage arrangements that you want. (If you take longer than your allotted time, points will be deducted.)

The judges will also be looking closely at how each musical number is performed.

They want to see how you sing and dance as a group. The group with the highest score will be selected as the grand champion. (Judging is points-based, so there may be a tie.)

Every aspect of your performance will be considered. The judges will give awards for best vocals, best male soloist, and best female soloist. Awards will also be given for best choreography, best set, best show design, and best costume. Sometimes they even give best band, best crew, and spirit awards.

Traveling to Perform

When you perform off campus or out of town, you will need to find a way to get there. You may want to ask someone in the glee club to act as your travel agent. This person will coordinate all of your travel arrangements whether they are near or far.

Sometimes it will be as simple as asking parents to drop you off and pick you up later. Or you can ask some of the

CHAPERONES

Most school districts require adult chaperones at student events. Nowadays if anyone will be in contact with students, they must complete a criminal background check. (This is the law in some states.)

In addition, the district may have its own forms for adult chaperones to complete. All of this information is kept on file in the office. Needless to say, it takes time to complete this paperwork. If you want someone to chaperone your event, ask at least a month ahead of time. It can take two to three weeks just to get the paperwork processed and approved.

juniors and seniors if they can drive your members to the event. (Using student drivers will depend on the laws in your state.) Carpooling works fine if your performances are close by.

If you need to travel outside of the city where you live, you may need to make more elaborate arrangements. The distance from your school to the event will determine which mode of transportation works best. If you have a small glee club, you may still be able to arrange a carpool for traveling to events that are just a few hours away. On the other hand, if you have a larger glee club it would probably be best to rent a bus. You may be able to use a school bus. Coach buses with air-conditioning, padded seats, and a bathroom are also available for rental for longer trips.

You can set up a carpool to help everyone travel to glee club events that are close by. Remember to observe the rules of the road and drive safely!

Traveling outside your region may require an airline ticket and a stay in a hotel. Hotels and airlines both offer group plans, so be sure to ask about this when you are making travel arrangements. Because you are booking a large number of airline seats and/or rooms, groups are usually offered a discount. At the same time, this price is discounted because they require you to pay for everyone with just two checks. The first check (or money order) is submitted when you book a group of airline tickets or hotel rooms. The second payment is made before airline tickets are issued or upon arrival at your hotel. In each case, only a single payment is made. It is up to you and your group to collect the funds to make these payments. For security purposes you will also be required to provide information about each person traveling with you.

Sharing the News

After each performance, share the news about your glee club. Share it at school and with your local media, the newspaper, and television station. Who will take care of this for you?

Your club will need a historian. Ask your historian to write up a short review of what happened and submit it to the school newspaper. Any big news, like placing at a competition, should be shared at morning announcements the next day. This news can also be sent to the local media. Keeping the media aware of what you are doing can result in news coverage outside of school.

Take lots of pictures at each event. Share them with the members of your glee club. Post them on your glee club Web page. You want to remember every single minute!

GLOSSARY

a cappella Music that is sung with voices without instruments.

audition A trial given to a performer as a test.

block To plan movement on a stage.

chaperone An older person who accompanies and supervises a group.

choral music Music sung by a choir.

choreography The art of composing a dance.

ensemble A group of musicians.

glee A song with different voice parts sung by three or more unaccompanied voices.

invitational A competition open only to invited guests.

mentor A counselor or teacher.

monies The plural of money.

producer A person who organizes and oversees an event for the stage.

publicity Information sent out to be noticed by the public.

rubric A set of rules to follow.

sponsor A person or company who pays for a program so it can advertise its product.

vendor A person or company that sells something.

venue The location of an event.

volunteer A person who performs a service without pay.

Alliance of Dance Notation Educators
Meadows School of the Arts
Southern Methodist University
P.O. Box 750356
Dallas, TX 75275-0356
(214) 768-3872
Web site: http://smu.edu/dancenotation
Sponsored by the Dance Notation Bureau, this organization provides
    teaching materials for dance students of all ages.

American Choral Directors Association (ACDA)
545 Couch Drive
Oklahoma City, OK 73102-2207
(405) 232-8161
Web site: http://acda.org
The ACDA is a nonprofit music education organization for excellence
    in choral music.

Finale National Show Choir Championships
Mind's Eye Conceptions
1216 Hardesty Boulevard
Akron, OH 44320
(800) 287-0532
Web site: https://www.facebook.com/group.php?gid=
        152166134812218
This four-day national championship competition for high school
    show choirs is held in the spring in New York City.

Harvard Glee Club
Holden Chapel, Harvard Yard
Harvard University

Cambridge, MA 02138
(617) 495-5730
Web site: http://www.harvardgleeclub.org
Founded in 1858, the oldest glee club in the United States is still
all male.

Showchoir Camps of America
P.O. Box 583
Naperville, IL 60566
(630) 663-4500
Web site: http://www.showchoircamps.com
This organization holds one-week summer camps for show choirs.

Show Choir Canada
736 Bathurst Street, Suite 100
Toronto, ON M5S 2R4
Canada
(855) 985-5000
Web site: http://www.showchoircanada.com
Twenty high school choirs from across Canada compete in this
national championship in Toronto.

Show Choir National Championship Series
FAME Events
7225 E. Hampton Avenue, Suite 127
Mesa, AZ 85209
(800) 289-6441
Web site: http://www.showchoirs.org
After a series of qualifiers, the top three show choirs at each event are
invited to compete in this high school national championship
in the midwestern United States.

Show Choir Nationals
3317 Winchester Road
Birmingham, AL 35226
(205) 305-8543
Web site: http://www.showchoirnationals.com
Twenty high school and middle school choirs from across the
    United States compete in this national championship at the
    Grand Ole Opry House in Nashville.

University of Michigan Men's Glee Club
P.O. Box 4037
Ann Arbor, MI 48106
(734) 764-1448
Web site: http://www.ummgc.org
Founded in 1859, this men's glee club is the second oldest in the
    United States.

Yale Glee Club
P.O. Box 201929
New Haven, CT 06520-1929
(203) 432-4136
Web site: http://www.yalegleeclub.org
Founded in 1863, this is one of the most traveled collegiate coed
    choruses in the world.

Web Sites

Due to the changing nature of Internet links, Rosen Publishing has
developed an online list of Web sites related to the subject of this
book. This site is updated regularly. Please use this link to access
the list:

http://www.rosenlinks.com/glee/perf

FOR FURTHER READING

Balser, Erin. *Don't Stop Believin': The Unofficial Guide to Glee*. Toronto, Canada: ECW Press, 2010.

Borg, Bobby. *The Musician's Handbook: A Practical Guide to Understanding the Music Business*. New York, NY: Billboard Books, 2008.

Chertkow, Randy. *The Indie Band Survival Guide: The Complete Manual for the Do-It-Yourself Musician*. New York, NY: St. Martin's Griffin, 2008.

Crossingham, John. *Learn to Speak Music: A Guide to Creating, Performing, and Promoting Your Songs*. Toronto, Canada: Owlkids, 2009.

Good Housekeeping. *The Great Bake Sale Cookbook: 75 Sure-fire Fund-raising Favorites*. New York, NY: Hearst Books, 2009.

Haring, Bruce. *How Not to Destroy Your Career in Music: Avoiding the Common Mistakes Most Musicians Make*. Los Angeles, CA: Lone Eagle, 2005.

Henderson, Anne T. *Beyond the Bake Sale: The Essential Guide to Family/School Partnerships*. New York, NY: New Press, 2007.

Lowell, Sophia. *Glee: The Beginning: An Original Novel*. New York, NY: Poppy, 2010.

Lowell, Sophia. *Glee: Foreign Exchange: An Original Novel*. New York, NY: Poppy, 2011.

Lowell, Sophia. *Glee: Summer Break: An Original Novel*. New York, NY: Poppy, 2011.

Oliver, Sarah. *The Completely Unofficial Glee A-Z*. London, England: John Blake Publishing, 2010.

Phillips, Pamelia S. *Singing for Dummies*. Hoboken, NJ: Wiley, 2010.

Ramone, Phil. *Making Records: The Scenes Behind the Music*. New York, NY: Hyperion, 2007.

Sennett, Frank. *FUNdraising: 50 Proven Strategies for Successful School Fundraisers*. Thousand Oaks, CA: Corwin Press, 2007.

Thall, Peter M. *What They'll Never Tell You About the Music Business: The Myths, the Secrets, the Lies* (& a Few Truths). New York, NY: Crown, 2010.

Thompson, Leah. *Behind Every Step: Have You Got What It Takes to Be a Choreographer?* Minneapolis, MN: Compass Point Books, 2009.

Williams, Anne-Marie. *Learn to Speak Dance: A Guide to Creating, Performing, and Promoting Your Moves.* Toronto, Canada: Owlkids, 2011.

Wilson, Leah. *Filled with Glee: The Unauthorized Glee Companion.* Dallas, TX: Smart Pop, 2010.

BIBLIOGRAPHY

Actor's Equity Association. "Guidelines for Dance Captains."
    2001. Retrieved October 5, 2011 (http://www.actorsequity.
    org/docs/production/Dance_captain_guidelines.pdf).

Allen, David. *Making It All Work: Winning at the Game of Work
    and the Business of Life*. New York, NY: Viking, 2008.

Baghai, Mehrdad. *As One: Individual Action, Collective Power*.
    New York, NY: Portfolio Penguin, 2011.

Brennan, Bridget. *Why She Buys: The New Strategy for Reaching the
    World's Most Powerful Consumers*. New York, NY: Crown, 2009.

Conrad, David. "Show Choir Audition Rubric." River Valley Music
    Association. Retrieved September 28, 2011 (http://www.
    windensemble.org/education/rubricshowchoir.htm).

Covey, Stephen R. *The 7 Habits of Highly Effective People:
    Restoring the Character Ethic*. New York, NY: Simon and
    Schuster, 1989.

Dance Notation Bureau. "Notation Basics." Retrieved October 5,
    2011 (http://www.dancenotation.org).

Fox, Jeffrey J. *How to Get to the Top: Business Lessons Learned at
    the Dinner Table*. New York, NY: Hyperion, 2007.

Green, Holly G. *More Than a Minute: How to Be an Effective
    Leader and Manager in Today's Changing World*. Franklin
    Lakes, NJ: Career Press, 2009.

Hawkins, Charlie. *Make Meetings Matter: Ban Boredom, Control
    Confusion, and Terminate Time-Wasting*. Franklin Lakes, NJ:
    Career Press, 2008.

Heath, Chip. *Made to Stick: Why Some Ideas Survive and Others
    Die*. New York, NY: Random House, 2007.

Heath, Chip. *Switch: How to Change Things When Change Is
    Hard*. New York, NY: Broadway Books, 2010

Levy, Reynold. *Yours for the Asking: An Indispensable Guide to
    Fundraising and Management*. Hoboken, NJ: John Wiley &
    Sons, 2008.

Maxwell, John C. *Mentoring 101: What Every Leader Needs to Know*. Nashville, TN: T. Nelson, 2008.

Meyers, Peter. *As We Speak: How to Make Your Point and Have It Stick*. New York, NY: Atria Books, 2011.

Passman, Donald S. *All You Need to Know About the Music Business*. New York, NY: Free Press, 2009.

Pearson, Timothy R. *The Old Rules of Marketing Are Dead: 6 New Rules to Reinvent Your Brand & Reignite Your Business*. New York, NY: McGraw-Hill, 2011.

Sperling, Jody. "Time Lapse Dance." 2009. Vocabulary Test. Retrieved September 28, 2011 (http://jodysperling.com/process/rehearsals/vocabulary-test).

Theater Student Handbook. "Positions of Responsibility Job Descriptions." Retrieved October 5, 2011 (http://theatre.uindy.edu/handbook/posofrespbody.htm).

Walker, Wendy. *Producer: Lessons Shared from 30 Years in Television*. New York, NY: Center Street, 2010.

INDEX

A

a cappella, 5, 11
auditions, 8, 18–23

B

bake sales, 43, 44
blocking, 29–30
booster clubs, 38

C

car washes, 44
chaperones, 51
choreography, 26–30, 51
costumes, 13, 34–35, 36, 51
Covey, Stephen, 9, 10
crew chief, 12, 31–32, 35

D

dance captains, 12, 28–29

F

Facebook, 15, 21
fund-raising, 36–38, 45–46
  bookkeeping and banking, 36–38,
    44–45
  frugal options for, 42–44
  sponsors, 39–40
  vendors, 41, 42
  volunteer sellers or service providers,
    40–41

G

garage sales, 44, 46
Glee, 4, 28

glee clubs

glee clubs
  history of, 4–5
  origin of name, 6
  positions, 12

H

Harvard Glee Club, 4
historian, 12, 53

J

judges, 20, 50, 51

L

labanotation, 29
lighting, 13, 33, 34

M

makeup, 35
materials, 13–14
mentors, 16, 18, 20, 23, 26
musicians, choosing, 8, 11, 13, 23–25
Myspace, 15, 21

P

performance venues
  competitions, 23, 47, 50–51, 53
  paid shows, 14, 49–50
  public service performances, 47, 49
  school, 47–48
permissions, 18
planning your production, 9–10
practice, 25
producer, 8–9, 14
props, 13, 33, 34
publicity, 13, 14–15, 21–23, 45–46, 53

R

rubric, 20
Rule of Seven, 23

S

school band, 13, 25
section leaders, 12, 23
sets, 34
sheet music, 13, 17, 18, 21
singers, choosing, 8, 10, 23
songs, choosing, 8, 17
Sperling, Jody, 30
stage crew, choosing, 8, 13, 31–34

T

travel agent, 12, 41
treasurer, 12, 36–38

trips, 36, 38, 51–53
Twitter, 15

U

University of Michigan Glee Club, 4

V

volunteers, 15, 31, 33, 40–41,
    42, 49

W

workshops, 20–21

Y

Yale Glee Club, 4
YouTube, 21, 28, 30

About the Author

Anastasia Suen is the author of more than one hundred books for children and adults. The daughter of a church cantor, she was in choir (and/or band) from elementary school until after college. Both of her children followed in her footsteps, culminating with her daughter singing in both the show choir and a state choir that toured Europe. Suen lives with her family in Plano, Texas.

Photo Credits

Cover, p. 30 Hill Street Studios/Blend Images/Getty Images; cover, back cover, interior graphics (stars, marquee) © istockphoto.com/Yap Siew Hoong; back cover, interior graphics (stage lights silhouette) Collina/Shutterstock.com; p. 5 Adam Rose/© Fox/courtesy Everett Collection; pp. 8, 48 © AP Images; p. 11 © David Joles/Star Tribune/ZUMA Press; p. 14 Comstock/Thinkstock; p. 17 iStockphoto/Thinkstock; p. 19 Milton Montengro/WorkbookStock/Getty Images; p. 22 auremar/Shutterstock.com; p. 24 PM Images/Stone/Getty Images; p. 27 Andrew Alfaro/MCT/Newscom; p. 32 Ableimages/Lifesize/Thinkstock; p. 34 Roman Sinichkin/Shutterstock.com; p. 37 Red Chopsticks/Getty Images; p. 39 Creatas/Thinkstock; pp. 43, 49 © Cindy Charles/PhotoEdit; p. 52 Jupiterimages/Brand X Pictures/Thinkstock.

Designer: Nicole Russo; Editor: Bethany Bryan;
Photo Researcher: Karen Huang